CW00674500

What Would a
Wicked Witch Do?

Pop Press is an imprint of Ebury Publishing
20 Vauxhall Bridge Road
London SW1V 2SA

Pop Press is part of the Penguin Random House group of companies
whose addresses can be found at global.penguinrandomhouse.com

Penguin
Random House
UK

Text © Pop Press 2024
Illustrations © Pop Press 2024

First published by Pop Press in 2024

www.penguin.co.uk

A CIP catalogue record for this book is available from the British Library

ISBN 9781529953046

Text by Susan Clark
Illustrations by Ollie Mann

Printed and bound in Great Britain by Clays Ltd, Elcograf S.p.A.

The authorised representative in the EEA is Penguin Random House Ireland,
Morrison Chambers, 32 Nassau Street, Dublin D02 YH68

Penguin Random House is committed to a sustainable future for our business, our readers
and our planet. This book is made from Forest Stewardship Council® certified paper.

MIX
Paper | Supporting
responsible forestry
FSC® C018179

What Would a
Wicked Witch Do?

POP PRESS

Contents

Introduction

This is a book of two magical halves. And the person who can decide which half steps forward on any given morning is you.

Will it be your inner Wicked Witch who strides forward to guide you through the day, week, month or even year? Or will your Good Witch nudge her out of the way for a while in order to sprinkle your life with magical stardust for the day, the week, the month or the rest of the year? Will you connect, today, more with the Earth (your Wicked Witch) or the Sky (your Good Witch)?

The decision really is yours.

Life is all about the journey and a big part of that journey is becoming skilled at integrating all parts of yourself. Nobody is all good, and sometimes even the Good Witch can be bad. Equally, nobody is all wicked. Dig deep into her story and you'll find goodness in the Wicked Witch and even a compassion for those less fortunate who may not be able to speak up or out for themselves.

With this book — which explores the characters and often hard-won wisdom of the two most famous witches of Oz — you can play with the light and the shadow in your own life and use the wisdom of each witch trope to navigate your way to lasting happiness (which really does only ever come from within). You can also explore which of your inner witches is coming out to play in both your work and your love life right now.

Check out the chapters on family and style and creating your own Coven (tribe) of supportive friends and see what you can learn about work and love and creativity from our two witches, who both have so much to offer.

They say when the student is ready, the teacher will come. Here, we have two teachers and the privilege of learning from both.

You'll pick up some handy magical skills along the way, learn how to cast a powerful spell or two, and by the time you've connected to both witches, you'll understand that in fairy tales, as in life, things are never all that they seem.

And that is precisely what makes it all so magical.

What Would a Wicked Witch Do?

In *The Wonderful Wizard of Oz* book, there were two sisters – the Wicked Witches of the East and the West. These two fearsome-looking hags had none of the redeeming qualities with which later versions of these characters were portrayed. That said, they were both powerful and not to be messed with. We've learned through later iterations of these iconic women, and through retellings of well-known stories as a whole, that there are two sides to every story. We have also discovered that there is much we can learn from these women — and the archetype of the witch — who stand in their power, even when the rest of the world won't like them for it.

Drawing on Wicked Witch wisdom means stepping to real empowerment, even if that requires becoming what other people see as 'the villain' of the story. This is wisdom for those who struggle to put their own needs first and who cannot seem to say no, even when they know someone is taking advantage of them.

You don't have to be mean to be a Wicked Witch, but you do have to put yourself first and stand up for yourself, whatever the cost. Yes, some people might pull away, but your true friends and family will stand by you. This archetype is all about staying true to herself. And it's not for no reason she's been a mainstay in fairy tales and mythology since the dawn of time. It is always the Wicked Witch who moves things on with either her magic, her trickery or her forthright way of saying and doing things.

Make no mistake, she's serious and deep and here to make a difference, especially for those who are oppressed or exploited. You can think of her as an activist and decide for yourself what cause you want to fight for when you channel your Wicked Witch powers; animal welfare, social justice, saving the planet?

Someone who embodies the magic and wisdom of the Wicked Witch is Elphaba – the green-skinned witch who is the protagonist of *Wicked* – but of course there have been many, many witches, good and bad, before her.

In the Slavic fairy tale of Baba Yaga, for example, we meet an embodiment of the Hag who is sometimes depicted as a nice old lady (nobody grows up wanting to just be nice!) who helps the hero, and sometimes as a ferocious villain from who you'd run a mile. Dark and light all rolled into one. And sometimes she is even portrayed as three sisters, rather than just one person.

Witches have always cropped up in fairy tales, and because these are stories of magic and nothing being quite as it first appears, it can be the case that the Wicked Witch turns out to be doing some good.

Is this something you would like to do too?

If so, read on …

Seven Wicked Witch Rules To Live By

Remember, with magic nothing is as it seems, which means sometimes the Wicked Witch in you will be doing good in all sorts of wonderful ways, but you should start with doing good for yourself. That way you'll have plenty of love and compassion left over for others.

1. Don't be afraid to step into your villain era and put your needs and self-care first.

2. Never compromise your values just to be accepted.

3. Never shrink yourself to fit the expectations of others. Being the best version of yourself means being the real you.

4. Remember, the strongest people have often overcome the biggest wounds.

5. Never fall in with the 'in' crowd. You don't need them.

6. Comparison is the thief of joy, so don't compare yourself to others.

7. Find a way, every day, to celebrate your uniqueness.

Family

The Wicked Witch values her independence, and as the truthteller in the family, she may find herself estranged from those who find her a bit much.

What this does is allow her to find her own path in life and to march to the beat of her own unique drum.

She doesn't follow the crowd or fall in with popular opinion just to keep the peace; she will speak out for herself and what she believes in. In doing this she can find her chosen family, those who respect and love her for who she truly is.

She is not defined by her family of origin and/ or their values but finds her own way in the world, knowing that if there is one person she can always rely on, it is herself.

Choosing self-love

Although *Wicked's* Elphaba is just one iteration of the 'Wicked Witch's trope, she is a good example of how we can transcend family wounds and life's other challenges to choose self-love. What her story tells us is that we can overcome the challenges we face through life and, like all the Wicked Witches through history, find our own voices.

Self-love is not the same as selfishness.

Self-love is the way we prioritise and take care of our own needs, which is when we then have the capacity to take care of others too.

What we learn from the Wicked Witch, is don't ever be afraid to be MASSIVE.

Choosing your family

The good news is that you really can choose the people you want to think of as your family – your soul sisters and brothers and uncles and aunts. And even your own witchy godmother.

You can think of this new tribe as your 'found' family.

Find the people who will love and respect and genuinely care for you. They will probably be like-minded folk who share the same values as you. And remember to be playful too. The Wicked Witch of the West had great fun with the flying monkeys that were both her friends and her allies.

Allies is a good word here. Who can you trust to fight your corner and support you when you stand up for yourself and what you believe in? These are the people who make up your found family.

'Family is what
you make it to be.'

'Finding your
soul sisters feels like
coming home.'

Coven

One of the joys of maturing is reaching the understanding that alongside the family you are born into — which you've had no say in — you will go on to create an equally important family and group of supportive people you might want to think of as your chosen tribe, or your Coven.

These are not the people your birth has just landed you with. They are those with whom you have chosen to share the journey of life – the good, the bad and the indifferent.

Your tribe consists of the people who know and love you for who you are, not who you think you have to be to fit in.

And sometimes these are the people (and the animals) you least expect them to be.

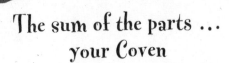

The sum of the parts ... your Coven

Covens make the magic stronger and more potent.

Think of that saying, 'the sum of the parts is greater than the whole'. That's the same for the unique group of witches that come together in a Coven, which then serves to make their spells stronger and their magic even more magical.

Bonding as one and making everyone feel accepted as they are is a big part of Coven lore, so there will be no need to hide who you really are from your fellow witches once you find each other.

Another joy of practising your magic in a group is that you will learn from each other, since you are likely to bring different strengths and skills to your gatherings.

Don't be afraid to step into the spotlight at Coven meetings and show just how powerful your Badass Witch magic is. No more hiding your light ....

Dust to Dust ...

In the original *Wizard of Oz* book, there were four witches, one for each of the cardinal directions: North, South, West and East. And it was the latter two who were said to be the more wicked, with the Wicked Witch of the West, the worst of all.

In the 1939 MGM film of the book, the Wicked Witch of the East went the way of all film villains and came to abrupt end when she was crushed under the weight of Dorothy's house, which had been picked up and hurled to Oz by a cyclone.

It was said this Wicked Witch was so very old that her body simply crumbled to dust and there was no blood on the ground where she fell because it had long ago dried up.

Is there anything that's dried up in your life? Anything that's no longer nourishing or sustaining? If so, maybe now would be a good time to let it go?

Once you've identified 'the thing' you would be happy to release back to the earth.

Don't forget to chant... 'Good riddance!'

'Friendships can be equally as important as romantic relationships.'

'The strength of a Coven
lies in its unity; together,
we are unstoppable.'

Style

*C*ue: Boots, earth, soil and mysterious shadowy shades.

If you want to channel your Wicked Witch then the dominant colour in your wardrobe will be black. Followed by green. And if you are going to push the boat out, maybe incorporate a hint of a fiery red lining into your cape.

A black pointy hat, a thick black coat or cape and killer pointed boots are the uniform of every Wicked Witch who has ever lived, and if you are going for gold, you'll want to throw in a scratchy black cat and large broomstick, too.

Every single element of this wardrobe is symbolic. You have chosen clothes that make you feel self-confident, empowered and strong. In other words, this is a style statement that leaves nobody in any doubt that you mean business and are here to get things done. So whether you're wearing all black or all pink, find those clothes that make you feel strong, sassy and independent and wear them with pride.

Breaking down bastions

Wicked witches don't give a stitch for fashion or trends. They are all about being and looking empowered.

The Oz witches made their debut appearances in 1900 when the book was first published. This was a time when the hems on women's dresses were starting to rise and although corsets were still in fashion, the restrictive dresses of bygone eras were gone. The suffragettes were making their mark – and not just with their more modern wardrobes, which allowed them to move more freely.

Billowing cloaks and pointed hats are a look from the style book of a grown and empowered woman. That doesn't mean you can't be sexy and feminine, but it does mean that you should explore what makes you feel powerful.

'Blending into the crowd would mean diminishing her own power, whereas recognising and exploiting that which makes her unique can get her to where she needs to be.'

'Visually, she always
has the sense of really
being grounded.'

Magic

The word magic refers to the ability to suddenly influence events using mysterious or supernatural forces.

Our Oz witches — good and bad — all take the study of magic and their own magical skills very seriously, treating it as an exquisite combination of science and art. The *Wicked* witches actually meet at university, but of course there are lots of witchcraft courses on offer online, so if you want to upskill, you shouldn't have to look too far to find a Wicked Witch mentor.

Of course, every self-respecting witch – wicked or otherwise – will have an animal 'familiar' who works alongside them, and whilst it is common to see a depiction of a witch with her black cat, why not think outside the box and find your own familiar for yourself? Look out for those creatures that cross your path in real life, in dreams or even on TV.

Imagine the fun you'll both have and the chaos you can create (just for fun) once you unleash your WW magical powers. That said, remember the Wiccan rule of three, which basically states be careful what you send out because it will boomerang back on you, three-fold. So, keep your wicked magic fun and harmless.

Smoke & Mirrors

Wicked Witch magic is nothing if not highly inventive. Here are a few ideas courtesy of the original Oz villains and their handy flying broomsticks.

Warning: However much fun this all sounds, do not try any of this at home!

- Magicking up sleep-inducing poppies to send people who are getting on your last nerve off to La La Land to give you some respite.

- Throwing fireballs to create a literal red smokescreen to hide what you're really up to behind the scenes.

- Spelling out sky-borne messages in black smoke with the end of your broomstick to threaten your foes (The WW of the West famously wrote '*Surrender Dorothy*' in black smoke above the skies of Oz.

- Training up a gang of wicked flying monkeys to carry out your dirty work and kidnap the enemy on your command.

- Making it rain indoors just to annoy (and soak through) people who have made you cross.

- Poison juicy-looking apples to 'eliminate' people

- Go around creating magical portals (doorways) to 'disappear people' who you don't like through to another dimension, where they will hopefully take up residence and stay!

- Create a sumptuous gingerbread home to lure small children into your lair

- Dance about (manically) in red shoes, because once upon a time people believed women who wore red shoes were secretly Wicked Witches!

Find the rituals
that work for you

Simple everyday acts can bring a little
magic into your life and it's important to
find the practices that empower you.

• Take a quiet moment in the morning
with your tea or coffee to be present.
What can you see, smell or hear?

• Remember to care for yourself as you set
out on the new day. Do you have a moment for
self-care? Why not apply some moisturiser to
your hands, or a serum to your hair or face?

• Take a walk around the block. Breathe in
the fresh air, notice the elements
and nature around you.

• Think about your intentions for the
day. What do you want from it?
Set your intentions, light a candle
and manifest the results.

Record your own rituals and practices here

_____

_____

_____

_____

_____

_____

_____

_____

_____

_____

'There's a little witch
in all of us.'

'Magic is a state of mind. It is often portrayed as very black and gothic, and that is because certain practitioners played that up for a sense of power and prestige. That is a disservice. Magic is very colorful. Of this, I am sure.'

Work &
Creativity

Job title: Activist

I n the original *Wizard of Oz* the Wicked Witch of the West, who has gone by many names over the years — including Theodora and Morella — is the archenemy of the heroine Dorothy and the allies she meets along the Yellow Brick Road, including Tin Man, Scarecrow and Cowardly Lion.

Power-hungry, she is more of a caricature depiction of a Wicked Witch than any of the iterations that followed. And her sole 'career' goal is to take possession of Dorothy's magical ruby red slippers so that she can control the Kingdom of Oz.

When Dorothy's house crash-landed in Oz, it fell directly onto the Wicked Witch of the East and killed her, and so in the original tale, the furious Wicked Witch of the West is on the warpath and out to avenge her sister's death.

The WW of the West has many witchy tricks in her workbag and is prone to throwing fireballs and disappearing in a cloud of red smoke when thwarted.

Thankfully, later versions of the Wicked Witches were more nuanced and by the time we get to Elphaba's character, we have a far more three-dimensional depiction. She is someone who works hard to achieve justice for all, and who is not just in the witchcraft business to manifest what she wants for herself.

Clearly, being a witch is all about your superpower. What would you say is yours?

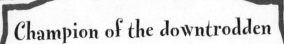

Champion of the downtrodden

The Wicked Witch was often a symbol of those who were being persecuted for being different and not fitting in. Being treated this way can lead to a real understanding of what it means and feels like to be treated as an outcast.

Women with power (especially those who were believed to be witches) were usually feared by men, and history tells of shocking eras where women were killed for no greater crime than knowing which hedgerow herbs could alleviate a fever and which would aid in childbirth.

These were the wise women of their times, who were regarded with suspicion as Wicked Witches simply because they could make a difference.

Hedgerow witches

It may be that you prefer to channel your own Wicked Witch as a solo practitioner, because although lots of witches enjoy being part of a Coven, many prefer to practise solo. These are known as Hedgerow Witches.

If you are working as a Hedgerow Witch, you may find allies showing up in the shape of animals that cross your path or appear in dreams. Start a dream journal and see if you can fathom how these allies can be of help in your working life. Get creative and ask yourself, what messages do they share? Study their lifestyles and habitats and see what learnings you can incorporate into the work version of you.

For example, if a guard dog keeps appearing, you might want to think about work teams and loyalties and keep a close eye on those you currently work alongside. Is someone taking the credit for your ideas or talking about you behind your back? Stay alert... and on guard.

'It's important to be
telling stories where
women are strong,
independent and driven.'

'You actually discover
that she's a wonderful
person and does
everything from the
goodness of her heart.'

Love

When it comes to matters of the heart, the Wicked Witch brings the same full force of her passions that she brings to everything else, but if you want a good relationship, the place to start is with yourself.

The Wicked Witch knows she needs to show up authentically for everything – including love. And that is, of course, what makes her such a force to be reckoned with.

She won't waste time on someone who does not deserve her in all her glory; she'd rather stay home with a good book of spells and a warm cat curled up on her lap until the right 'one' comes along.

She is the epitome of a woman who knows her worth, who is not about to compromise, fade into the background or shrink-wrap herself for the sake of a romantic relationship. And she also understands that love can express itself and come in many different forms, including friendships.

So if you're ready for a serious and meaningful relationship it might be time to unleash your Wicked Witch, because she's not messing about, in love or life, and when she loves, she loves with all her being, not just her heart.

Witches in love

If there's one thing a Wicked Witch will never compromise on it is love; romantic or otherwise. The biggest teaching we can take from the way a Wicked Witch conducts her life is that love starts inside a person with love for themselves, and that this is soon followed by self-acceptance.

Self-acceptance leads to more self-esteem and the latter is a great foundation for all relationships, including romantic ones.

When you finally accept yourself, you radiate self-confidence – and there is nothing more attractive to the people around you.

You may not be on the lookout for love, but as soon as you find meaning in loving and accepting yourself, love will find its way to your door.

Wicked's Elphaba ended up marrying a boy she first met at university but not until she'd accepted herself – green skin and all – and made peace with being different. As soon as that happened, she fell in love and had the happy fairy tale ending she never dreamed…

'They both give
each other a deeper
sense of themselves
and a safe space.'

'Long seen as a symbol of otherness, witchcraft has become a way for queer folk to transform their difference into a superpower.'

What Would a
Good Witch Do?

Acknowledgements

p21 from *Psychology Today* website, article 'The Families We Choose', no named credit but reviewed by the *Psychology Today* staff, p23 from *A Life in Progress* website, article 'Finding your soul sisters feels like coming home' by Krista O'Reilly-Davi-Digui published 22 June 2016, p21 from the article *'Friends 'For Good' Wicked: A New Musical and the Idealization of Friendship'* by Valerie Lynn Schrader (*Communication and Theater Association of Minnesota Journal* (CTAMJ) Fall 2013), p28 Bookey website, '5 Key Lessons from The Coven' (no named author credited) *The Coven* is written by Lizzie Fry (also known as LV Hay) and published by Sphere Books (21 February, 2021), p35 from Broadway Inbound website, 'Broadway's Most Iconic Designs: A Look At the Creative Process Behind the Designs'. No named author. (26 June 2023), p36 V&A website, 'Elphaba Shiz Wicked '2003 (designed) Collections listing with image of the outfit, p36 from Showbusiness Insights website blog, 'The Extraordinary Cost of Elphaba's Costume', (4 May, 2014) no specific author credited, p38 from *Playbill* website, article 'How Wicked Costume Designer Susan Hilferty Put Her Own Twist on Oz' by Adam Hetrik, (1 April 2018), p37 from Skilful Conversation website, blog article 'Life Lessons from Musicals (Part 1: Wicked)' by Catherine Brown (no date of publication given), p44 from Ulysses press website, article 'Spell Jar Guide: Primary Steps and Recipe Guide to Manifest self Confidence' (22 August 2023) taken from the book *Spell Jars for the Modern Witch: A Practical Guide for Crafting Spell Jars for Abundance, Luck, Protection and More* by Mierva Siegal, p49 from Brainy Quote website, 'Alan Moore Quotes' page, Article Go Hollywood? Never by Geoff Boucher*Los Angeles Times* September 2008, p48 from Screenrant website, article 'Practical Magic: 20 Best Quotes, Ranked' by Amanda Bruce (19 June, 2024), p55 from YourTango website, article, 'What It Means To Belong to A 'Coven' (And How To Create Your Own)' by Colleen Fogarty (24 March, 2023), p56 from In Common website, interview article, 'In Conversation with Stars Sarah O'Connor (Glinda) and Laura Pick (Elphaba)' no specific author credited (29 April, 2024), p57 from *Total Girl* (Australia) website interview article 'Interview: Wicked The Musical', this interview is with Jemma Rix who was playing Elphaba in the stage production in Melbourne, there is no author credit or date for the article, p65 from *Dazed* website, article, 'How witchcraft has become a safe haven for the LGBTQ+ community' by Amelia Abraham (30 October 2019), from IMDb website citing the American Broadcasting Company's TV series, *Once Upon A Time*, episode called *Kansas*, Season 3, (2014), p17 from the IMBd website listing citing the musical film *The Wiz* (1978) which was based on the book, *The Wiz* (an adaptation of *The Wonderful Wizard of Oz*) by William F. Brown with lyrics by Charlie Smalls and made by Motown Productions, p16 from ABC's TV series (2011–2018) *Once Upon a Time in Oz*, episode 7, *The Defenders of Oz*, p27 from the MGM Technicolour film, *The Wizard of Oz (1939)* starring Judy Garland and directed by Victor Fleming, p32 from The Met website, '*Junon'* House of Dior Collections Listing, p32 from *The Hollywood Reporter* website, article 'See the 1949 Dior Gown That Inspired Anya Taylor-Joy's 2024 Oscar's Look' by Degemn Pener (13 March, 2024), p32 from *Playbill* website, article, 'Wicked on Broadway by the Numbers' by Ruthie Fierberg (29 October, 2018), p33 from Perspex website, article 'Gilbert Adrian and his work at MGM Studios' no specific author credited (30 July, 2019), p33 from Bonhams website, pre-sale catalogue listing, 'A Glinda the Good test wand from the Wizard of Oz,' (10 December, 2019), p34 from the School of Self-Image website, Podcast by Tonya Leigh, 'The Importance of a Style Statement' episode 299, p35 from from *Playbill* website, article 'How Wicked Costume Designer Susan Hilferty Put Her Own Twist on Oz' by Adam Hetrik, (1 April 2018), p42 from Ulysess press website, article 'Spell Jar Guide: Primary Steps and Recipe Guide to Manifest self Confidence' (22 August 2023) taken from the book *Spell Jars for the Modern Witch: A Practical Guide for Crafting Spell Jars for Abundance, Luck, Protection and More* by Mierva Siegal, p39–40 from the Disney Fandom website, listing for Glinda the Good, 1.3 Powers and abilities, (no author credits), p44 from Jon Finch's Finchmagician website, blog article, '50 of the Best Magic Quotes' by Jon Finch, p53 from *The Atlantic* website, article 'The Wizard of Oz invented the "Good Witch"' by Pam Grossman (25 August, 2019), p51 from Wikipedia citing a comment made by the fictional character, General Guph talking about Glinda in *The Emerald City of the Oz* book by L. Frank Baum, p60 from Jessica Baum's beselffull.com website and blog, article 'How Can Glinda the Good Witch Help You Avoid a Toxic Relationship?' by Jessica Baum (no publication date); p61 from the Florida State University Writing Resources English Department website essay, 'The Wizard of Oz: More Than Just A Children's Story' by Lauren Houlberg exploring the key archetypes in the fairy tale.

What Would a Good Witch Do?

POP PRESS

Contents

What Would a Good Witch Do?

Y ou know those days when you wake up and you're in love with the world and everyone and everything in it? It feels like life itself is a magical fairy tale and all you would have to do is wave your diamond-tipped wand and the whole world would be put right and everyone would be happy.

This is a very Good Witch day!

In the original *The Wonderful Wizard of Oz* book there were two Good Witches that later versions of the story mashed into the one Good Witch who we all know as Glinda.

Superficially, Glinda is so positive and radiant that everyone wants to be her friend, so if you're having one of those days when everything seems to be going your way, fairy tale Glinda is probably hovering close by in another dimension.

In this half of the book, you'll discover more about the powers of a Good Witch but also understand that nobody can be good all the time and that, as always with magic, there is more to a witch, good or wicked, than meets the eye.

Seven Good Witch Rules To Live By

Remember, with magic nothing is as it seems, which means sometimes the Good Witch in you will need to think outside of the box to leave her mark in the world.

1. If you can lend a hand, put down your diamond-tipped wand for a second and lend Hands?

2. Remember, there's never been an 'i' in the word team.

3. If someone doesn't believe in themselves *show* (don't tell them) that you have enough belief for you both.

4. When you wake each morning think of one of the virtues you'd like to embody all day. Take your pick from patience, kindness, charity, faith and prudence. Prudence (being careful) is a good one!

5. As a Good Witch you already believe in a benevolent universe, one that is kind and loving and has enough to go around for everyone. So don't let anyone persuade you otherwise.

6. Always use your magical powers for the greater good (not just your own dreams and desires). Remember that anything you send out can boomerang back three-fold, so don't misuse the power that has been entrusted to you.

7. Love your life. Love other people – especially the ones who are trickier to like, let alone love – and always open the doors for those less fortunate than you.

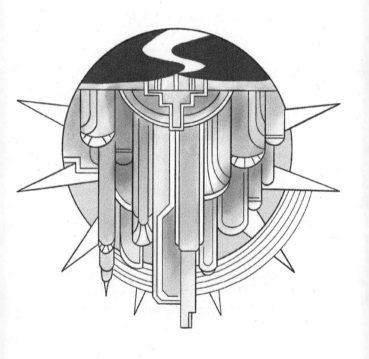

Family

Glinda is beautiful. Glinda is good. Glinda, in the *Wicked* books, is re-imagined as the pampered daughter of middle-class Gillikinese parents. She comes from a stable family living in the market town of Frottica, in the Pertha Hills of Gillikin, which is in the Northern province of Oz. Glinda's father is Highmuster Arduenna, the town leader, and her mother is Larena Upland, which means on the maternal side Glinda comes from Upland wealth and nobility.

Not surprisingly, Glinda's upbringing has meant that social standing, along with beauty and fashion, are all super important to her, and sometimes, despite being the 'good' witch, even more important than doing what is right.

In short, she can be a snob and is obsessed with people knowing that she comes from the Upper Uplands and has a noble heritage.

In *Dorothy and the Wizard of Oz*, an animated children's TV series, Glinda has a twin sister, Melinda the Mean, who is always trying to make her look bad in front of other people. Although Melinda has dark hair and a dark bubble that she flies around in, she has the magical powers to change her colouring and that of the bubble so she can pretend to be Glinda.

So, Glinda, might be a Good Witch but she is no stranger to sibling rivalry, spite, snobbery and jealousy.

When we first meet Glinda in any of the Oz versions where she plays a major role, we meet a beautiful and soft woman who is actually hiding a sharp intelligence. So another thing we can learn from Glinda is not to judge a book by its cover — or a witch by her pink gown, silver tiara and sparkly diamond-tipped wand.

Learning from
the ancestors

Go back just four generations (about 100 years before your birth) and you have 30 great-great-grandparents – that's 30 people who have passed some of their DNA and personality traits that, not which down through the maternal and paternal lines to create the unique human being that is you.

Same for Glinda and all the other Good Witches out there.

See if you can find out more about those distant ancestors. Is there anyone still alive who can share some of their life stories with you? Look for those Good Witch traits which have passed down the maternal or paternal lines to you.

'Only YOU can shape your destiny. But if you believe you're evil, then that is what you'll become.'

'Home is a place we all must find, child. It's not just a place where you eat or sleep. Home is knowing. Knowing your mind, knowing your heart, knowing your courage.'

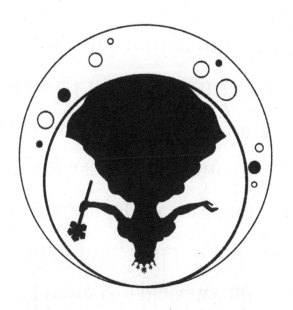

Coven

Y
ou can't choose your family, but you can absolutely choose your friends, and if you choose wisely, these will be the folk that travel life's path with you, sharing the ups and downs of the adventure.

You can think of these people as your trusted tribe or your very own Coven.

Friendship lies at the heart of *Wicked*, a story that is not only about magic, but also the forging of a deep but unlikely friendship between two young women who are as different as two women can be.

Witch Glinda is pretty, popular, flighty and hides her intelligence. Elphaba is solemn, down to earth, talented and disinterested in all the

things Glinda cares about, including looking good and attracting boys.

There are many learnings to be had from witnessing an unlikely friendship that is as deep as any romantic relationship – and maybe that is the primary take-home: that our friends are as important as our lovers, and sometimes they will be around and in our lives a lot longer than those we romance.

A Sisterhood

When she talks about the 'Sisterhood of Witches', Glinda is talking about creating that group of people or tribe who will stand in and compensate for the flaws of birth family.

These are the people we have some kind of soul contract to meet up with in this life or the next to share the journey of life and support each other through its highs and lows.

When the
magic happens

Scientists talk about something called
resonance, which is a kind of magical energetic
exchange and understanding that takes place –
without words – between two humans. This
explains why you may discover after you have
become friends that some of your Coven have
very similar childhood stories to yours.

And we also know that we can affect
and regulate the biology of anyone we are in
close proximity to, which is why hanging out
with your true friends – or the Sisterhood, as
Glinda would say – will leave you feel calm
and heard and appreciated and loved and just
somehow so much better for the conversation
and the connection.

Your Coven

The word Coven comes via Old French from the Latin word, *convenium*, which in turn comes from *convenire*, which means 'assemble'.

Historically, a Coven also referred to a group of 3 (minimum) and 13 (ideally).

Who do you most like to assemble or gather with? Try to name at least three people, or more if more come to mind.

What values do you all share? Kindness? Empathy? A willingness to put yourselves out for one another?

These are the people in your Good Witch Coven.

'I'm Glinda and this is Locasta. Welcome to the Sisterhood of Witches.'

'And so, what the
Munchkins want to know
is, are you a Good Witch
or a Bad Witch?'

Style

Cue: Light, bubbles & air

Glinda is a real girly-girl and likes to look pretty and feminine at all times. In the original *Wizard of Oz* book, her hair is flaming red and cascades down her back (which might just be a clue to those more fiery parts of her personality that she likes to hide), but when the writer Gregory Maguire came along to write *Wicked: the Life and Times of the Wicked Witch of the West*, he changed Glinda's hair to blonde.

Whatever your hair colour, you can channel Glinda's iconic style with a quick and easy makeover

of your wardrobe and send out that same signal that you like to look your best, even if it's just to put the bins out or take the dog for a walk in the park!

Your Glinda wardrobe will be full of pretty pastels – think soft pinks and baby blues – cosy cashmeres and floaty chiffons. There are no hard edges or scruffy boho vibes to this look and not a single pair of baggy jeans in sight.

The 'Bubble' dress

The beautiful 'bubble' ballgown-style dress that Glinda favours is based on a gorgeous haute couture garment designed in 1949 by Christian Dior.

Known as the 'Junon' dress it is named after Juno who was the goddess of marriage, women, the sky and all the stars of heaven, and whose sacred animal was the peacock (or Hera) in Greek mythology, whose sacred animal was the peacock and who was the Goddess of marriage, women, the sky and all the stars of heaven.

Dior's design concept was to capture the magnificent luminescence of a peacock's spectacular plumage and, so he designed a strapless bodice with a sumptuous skirt made of ombréed blue/green petals (feathers), which shimmer just like peacock feathers but without the 'eyes'.

The original dress, which was designed to be worn at grand galas, is part of the permanent costume collection at the de Young Museum in San Francisco. And it was clearly the inspiration for actress Anya Taylor-Joy's 2024 Oscar awards gown, with its delicate shell-like silk-tulle scales on the skirt and shimmering sequinned bodice.

Glinda's bubble dress has a staggering 68,200 sequins, so you might want to get started on yours!

Sparkly accessories

Glinda's favourite accessories might be a wand and a hair clip that looks like a star (or an off-centre tiara) and yours a sequinned smart phone cover and shimmering tote bag, but the sparkly glam-squad vibe will be the same.

In the 1939 film, *Wizard of Oz*, Glinda's original wand was designed by MGM Studios' costume designer, Gilbert Adrian, and made from clear rhinestones. Sadly, the original wand failed to sparkle in glorious technicolor and, so the designer went back to the drawing board and used brightly coloured stones instead.

Although two known copies of the original Glinda were made, nobody knows what happened to either, but in 2019, a stand-in silver 'wardrobe test wand' that had been used on set sold at a Bonhams auction for over $400,000.

Think about how the wand was changed to make more of an impact on celluloid. What might you need to change about yourself to be better seen and heard?

'The truth is everyone has style. But not everyone has purposeful style.'

'Glinda is light,
and bubbles, and air.
She's always the lightest
person in the scene.'

Magic

No self-respecting Good Witch would step out of the house – let alone into any magical space – without her trusty wand. In the 1939 film *The Wizard of Oz*, Glinda's wand was diamond-tipped and could be used in a flourish to set fire to something that needed destroying or to block would-be attackers from coming any closer.

But Glinda has more than a magical wand up her chiffon sleeves. Here are a few of her tricks and charms — all of which made her one of the most powerful sorceresses in the land of Oz.

- **Telekinesis:** The Good Witch can move objects just by pointing her diamond-tipped sparkly wand at them.

- **Hydrokinesis:** She can also conjure a thick white fog veil that she can use both offensively and defensively. It is particularly useful when wanted to 'disappear' on an advancing enemy.

- **Levitation:** Just like all serious practitioners of magic, Glinda can levitate and move herself through the air at will.

- **Bubble flight:** Glinda's preferred mode of transport is a protective bubble and she can conjure these out of the water in the clouds overhead so that her allies can move around safely too.

- **Magic blasts:** These emanate from the tip of her wand and can be used in all sorts of emergencies to deter attackers or set fire to things.

- **Kiss of protection:** A kiss on the forehead from Glinda would protect you from the bad magic coming your way from the Wicked Witches.

The need to diversify

In truth, all of Glinda the Good's magical powers come from her wand. She is powerless if parted from it and will die if it is ever broken. This makes her very vulnerable.

If you are in Good Witch mode, you might want to think about the ways in which you can diversify your magical and life skills, so you are less dependent on one trick and more resilient in the face of life's challenges.

Maybe add a little spell work into the mix, maybe join a Coven so you are less exposed, and maybe update your magical toolkit for the 21st century with, say, a digital wand (and a handy spare at home).

Find the rituals that work for you

Simple everyday acts can bring a little magic into your life, and it's important to find the practices that empower you.

- Take a quiet moment in the morning before you get out of bed. In your cosy place of rest, what can you see, smell or hear?

- Remember to care for yourself as you set out on the new day. Do you have a moment for self-care? Take time to pick out an item of clothing or an accessory that adds some sparkle to your day.

- The simple act of introducing a positive scent into your space or onto your clothes can set you on a powerful path. Which are the scents that make you feel good? .

- Take a walk around the block. Breathe in the fresh air and look to the sky. What do you see there?

- Think about your intentions for the day. What do you want to give today? Who do you want to help? Set your intentions, light a candle and manifest the results.

Record your own rituals
and practices here

'Magic touches people in
the way great art does.
It lets them see the world
with new eyes.'

'I always write "Magic Potion" on my perfume bottles, so when I use them, it feels magical. I make spells in the morning when I put them on.'

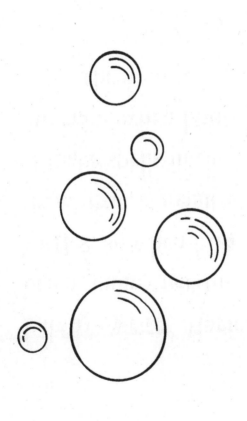

Work & Creativity

Job title: Fairy Godmother/ Pyschotherapist

I n the original book and again in the 1939 film *The Wonderful Wizard of Oz*, Glinda, the Good Witch, had an important job to do – she acted as a kind of fairy godmother to poor lost orphan Dorothy, guiding her to the Wizard of Oz and helping her find her way back home to her aunt and uncle in Kansas.

So, in a way, Glinda was one of the first Jungian-style therapists.

She understood her job was not to 'fix' Dorothy but to show her that she already had everything she needed inside her to believe in herself enough to find her own way home.

In the 1972 unofficial sequel to the iconic 1939 film, which was called *Journey Back to Oz*, we learn that Glinda comes from the fairy people, so the job title fairy godmother really does apply.

Finding your
fairy godmother

Glinda likes to think the best of everyone and champion them to find their self-belief.

Who does this for you?

Is there a former teacher, a friend, an aunt or another family member who always champions you? This person is likely to be older than you, with more life experience tucked under their belt, so cast your net wide and see who your true champion might be.

Call them your fairy godmother/father, your best cheerleader or just a Good Witch, but if you do have someone who supports you like this then you are lucky – hang on to him or her. And if you don't, make it your mission to get out there and find them. You'll never regret it.

Creative genius

In the 1986 animated version of *The Wonderful Wizard of Oz*, Glinda is not above using trickery to defeat her arch enemy, Mombi, who had once been the Wicked Witch of the North but is now a lowly old hag.

Mombi turns herself into a dragon to escape the Emerald City and whatever fate Glinda has in mind for her, but not to be outwitted, Glinda turns herself into an Eagle to pursue her. Eventually, Glinda uses all her powers to turn Mombi away from her bad intentions and make her a good person.

We can think of this as shapeshifting work.

If you were to shift shape and become another creature or being for a day, what or who would you be and why? And what do you think you would discover about yourself from such a major transformation?

'She commands the spirits of the air.'

'She was arguably the first American pop-culture figure to prove that, despite their reputation for diabolical antics, witches could be benevolent beings.'

Love

The original version of Glinda the Good was a more mature woman who relishes the role of fairy godmother and who is said to love everyone and want the best for all she meets. By the time we get an evolution of her in the form of Glinda from *Wicked*, her character has changed a bit, and what we see — the Good Girl — is not necessarily what we get, because she can be sneaky and mean.

However, let's leave sneaky and mean over in the shadows of our Wicked Witch and focus here on love and light for all.

Divine Feminine and Mother Earth are both great resources for us to turn to when we need extra support and making a connection to both will help you keep your Good Witch nature well-nourished and on track, whatever the challenges that come your way.

Love & romance

Romantic love is marvellous and if you are unleashing your inner Glinda you will, more than most, relish being swept off your fairy feet.

Your Wicked Witch shadow knows these feelings never last but must transmute to something more realistic for that love to become meaningful, but your Good Witch simply doesn't care because she's just in love with being in love.

There is nothing that makes you feel more alive, so we may as well indulge her.

Make a list in your journal of how being madly in love changes everything you see, hear, intuit, smell and touch. All the senses...

Love & compassion

The reason the Good Witch loves everyone is because her heart is full of compassion. Another way to think of this wonderful quality is that she has enormous empathy for the suffering of others and wants to do whatever she can to help relieve their misery.

Empathy is the key word here. Notice this is not the same as sympathy. When you feel sympathy, you remain 'outside' the field of someone's suffering and make all the right noises but somehow manage to avoid their pain rubbing off on you. When you have empathy, you will dive right in, hold their hand and simply say, 'I'm here for you'.

As you hone your Good Witch qualities, make empathy your goal and start your journey to that destination with kindness, remembering that kindness is always a choice. You can do or say something kind or not. It is always up to you.

In your journal, think of three times in the recent past you have been kind. How does this make you feel about yourself?

Now be scrupulously honest with yourself and list three occasions when you were not as kind as you might have been. How do you feel about yourself when you reflect those choices now?

'By filling yourself up
with love and compassion,
you have love to give
others… without
exhausting yourself.'

'Glinda the Good Witch represents the Mother archetype because she looks out for Dorothy.'

Flip from Good Witch

To Wicked Witch